COMMUNICATING WITH DIGNITY AND CURIOSITY

COMMUNICATING WITH DIGNITY AND CURIOSITY

The Peacemaker's Handbook for Creating and Sustaining Peace

ROBYN SHORT

goodmedia
PRESS

ALSO BY ROBYN SHORT

Prayers for Peace

Peace in the Workplace

Peace People

GoodMedia Press

An imprint of goodmedia communications, llc

25 Highland Park Village, 100-810

Dallas, Texas 75205

Cover design by Lindsey Bailey

Book design by GoodMedia Press

The text in this book is set in Fanwood.

Manufactured in USA.

978-1-7327046-2-6

CONTENTS

1. Introduction   1
2. Basic Human Needs Theory   3
3. Wheel Of Conflict   11
4. The Dignity Model   23
5. Engaging In Conflict With Dignity and Curiosity   31
6. Bringing It All Together   39

Notes   43
About the Author   47

INTRODUCTION

W hat causes us to get into conflict? What prevents us from being able to navigate conflict productively? How might we create systems of sustainable peace? These are the questions that led me to pursue an academic and professional career in peace-building.

Both the conflict resolution field and the field of peace-building lean toward reactive responses to conflict. In my work as a peacemaker, I am intensely curious about how we might develop systems that promote and sustain peace. I am interested in cultivating peaceful societies that support and nurture human development, which include the peaceful resolution of conflicts.

To understand human behavior, it is critical to know that the human brain is wired for survival. We are hardwired to perceive and respond to threats, and throughout human history, we have done this through conflictful and often violent means.

Humans have existed on Earth and have been in a process of

continuous change for more than 200,000 years, and the modern form of humans has been evolving for more than 50,000 years.

This process of evolution and continuous change has largely been a result of humans adapting to changes in the environment. External forces served as the catalyst for human evolution. Humans changed because the environment around them changed. Continuous change served as a mechanism for survival — adapt to the evolving environment or risk extinction.

For the first time in human history, modern humans have the knowledge, skills and intellectual capability to choose the destiny of humanity by intentionally shaping human evolution rather than reactively evolving to changes in our environment. Internal forces, rather than external forces exclusively, can now serve as the catalyst of human evolution.

This small handbook is an homage to the peace-building theorists and practitioners who have shaped my thinking, my studies, my work, and my understanding of how we as individuals can shift our thinking and our actions in order to forge a path toward a more peaceful society.

If this handbook inspires you to learn more, please browse the Notes section in the back of the book, so that you can take a deeper dive into the works mentioned throughout this handbook. Together, we can create human systems that support and sustain peace.

2

BASIC HUMAN NEEDS THEORY

The era immediately following World War II was a time period of optimism in academia as it related to the social sciences and the role the social sciences might play in solving some of the world's most complex social problems and persistent human problems, including issues related to conflict, war, and peace. Social scientists, of disparate backgrounds, were eager to apply new knowledge via a multi-disciplinary approach to pressing critical issues, especially pertaining to social, industrial and international conflict in pursuit of a more peaceful world. Because of the disparate background of many of these scholar-practitioners, there was a lack of cohesion in terms of theory and practice. Ideas were often drawn from social psychology, including knowledge about misperceptions, cognitive dissonance, dehumanization, and commitment theory; from group dynamics such as role theory and group think; industrial relations knowledge such as concession-convergence bargaining, intra-group cohesion; and from international relations knowledge such as escalation spirals and nonviolent direct action.[1] A process was often deemed as successful if it led to some form of positive change in the participants and new ideas about possible options for the future emerged. A true theoretical basis for arguing that intractable conflicts could be resolved by these methods was missing. As a result, a revived interest in Abraham Maslow's hierarchy of needs arose.

Maslow's theory of human needs asserts that all people possess "a number of basic needs and that the frustration of these needs would lead to conflictful behavior and even to organized (or disorganized) violence."[2] (Note: For the purposes of this paper, violence is defined as being present when individuals are influenced in such a way that their actual somatic and mental realizations are below their potential.[3]) According to Maslow, these needs are hierarchical in nature — one need must be met before the next, higher need, can be addressed — and follow a developmental, stages of growth sequence. Typically portrayed as a pyramid, Maslow's human needs include: 1) physiological needs; 2) safety and security; 3) love and belonging; 4) esteem; 5) self-actualization.[4]

Basic Human Needs Theory, originally developed by renowned conflict scholar John Burton, grew out of Maslow's Hierarchy of Needs theory. For Burton, basic human needs were "fixed, ontological, and universal."[5] Where Maslow posited that human needs are hierarchical, Burton argued that human needs are sought simultaneously, intensely, and relentlessly. Human needs are truly the very basic needs that are at the core of the human experience and that humans require to thrive and achieve a sustainable state of peace. (See Figure 1)

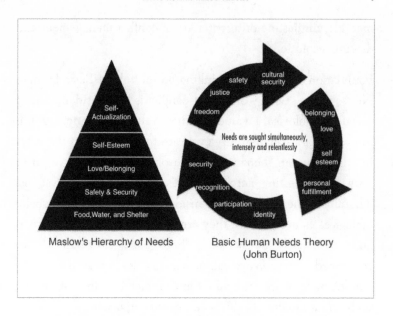

Fig. 1 / The image on the right reflects a combination of both Maslow's assertion of human needs with Burton's human needs.

Burton asserts that any conflict that has its roots in the violation or frustration of basic human needs is what he referred to as "deeply-rooted conflict." In contrast, a disagreement that has its foundation in less deeply rooted interests such as commercial or industrial interests is understood to be "disputes." Disputes may be resolved utilizing typical negotiation and mediation interventions; whereas, conflicts rooted in frustrated human needs are not amenable to compromise and/or negotiation tactics. Conflicts must be addressed via "problem-solving workshops," wherein the goal is to gain understanding of all parties and to explore ways in which all parties' needs can be met. Herein lies the differentiation of conflict management and dispute resolution.[6]

Foundational to Burton's thinking on the role of Basic Human Needs in the etiology of violent conflict is his considerations of social-psychological values. The values operate within individual and small-group levels are fundamental to the ways in which humans behave and, Burton asserts, are universal in terms of operating across cultures and ideological systems. Therefore, one might even consider these values to be socio-biological values because they are reflective of biological drives and biological motivations. Socio-biological values are concerned with the survival, personality development and self-maintenance of the individual and/or small group within any social environment. To this point, Burton argues that:[7]

A hypothesis that there are socio-biological values ... serves to explain the patently *continuing struggle* for participation and freedom to develop personality within a social environment ... the *persistent demand* for the independence of nations, and for identification of groups within states.

Burton's perspective on the importance of socio-biological values as the key drivers of human behavior, especially behavior oriented around conflict, eventually shifted toward a theory based on needs. Originally influenced by Maslow, Burton's thinking evolved to include the work of sociologist Paul Sites.

In contrast to Maslow's hierarchy of needs, Sites argued that there are eight needs, all of which hold equal importance and none of which are contingent upon the other. Sites' eight human needs, all of which are required to achieve a state of harmony and peace, consist of the following: 1) consistency in response; 2) stimulation; 3) security; 4) recognition; 5) distributive justice; 6) rationality and the appearance of rationality; 7) meaning; 8) control. To this list of eight needs, Burton added a ninth, role defense — "the protection of needs once they have been acquired."[8] Site's original list and Burton's reframing of it eventually evolved into a revised list of Basic Human Needs: 1) identity; 2) participation; 3) recognition; and 4) security. Burton asserts that each of these are an "ontological part of the human development process."[9] Foundational to both the values approach and the needs approach is Burton's argument that, "certain needs will be pursued, regardless of any force that might be used by authorities."[10]

Burton's implementation of Basic Human Needs Theory manifested as "analytical problem-solving facilitated conflict resolution."[11] The underlying assertion of problem-solving is that conflict is rarely, if ever, about the actual content of the conflict and rather about the frustration of one or more of the basic human needs. Therefore, rather than orient negotiation and mediation around the content of the conflict, the Basic Human Needs facilitator encourages the parties to bring to the surface their underlying motivation — the fulfillment of their needs.[12] The chronic frustration and violation of human needs can lead the frustrated actors to force their way into the consciousness of society via terrorism and other forms of extreme violence. In others words, violence can be perceived as an extreme alert that human needs are in a chronic state of violation.

Provention

An aspect of Burton's Basic Human Needs theory that makes it so attractive to the field of peace-building is the concept of *provention*. Johan Galtung defines peace as "the absence /reduction of violence of all kinds." He also explains that, "Peace is nonviolent and creative conflict transformation." He asserts that for both definitions, the following also holds true: "Peace work is work to reduce violence by peaceful means."[13]

Provention is of paramount importance to the work of peace-building because it takes into account both conflict prevention measures and measures to ensure the sustainability of peace. Burton coined this term as a means of encapsulating the concept of "prevention of the undesirable event by removing its causes, and by creating conditions that do not give rise to its causes."[14] Burton contrasts *provention* to *prevention*: "*pro*vention [signifies] taking steps to remove [underlying] sources of conflict, and more positively to promote conditions in which collaborative and valued relationships control behaviors."[15]

Provention is dependent upon proactive strategies, and humans tend to be reactive creatures. That stated, Burton's Basic Human Needs Theory offers a framework from which policymakers, community leaders, organizational leaders, etc. can affect positive social change in which "relationships are sustained by legitimate mechanisms of reciprocated support and not by coercive measures or by elites, by virtue of their own authority."[16]

Many conflict scholars and practitioners see Burton's Basic Human Needs Theory as incomplete. However, Basic Human Needs Theory has served as a strong foundation for additional theoretical explorations. The next two sections examine Bernard Mayer's "Wheel of Conflict" as well as Donna Hick's "The Dignity Model" as important additional elements of conflict resolution and peace-building.

3

WHEEL OF CONFLICT

B ernard Mayer is a conflict resolution theorist, scholar, and practitioner who positions human needs at the center of all conflicts. Mayer developed the "Wheel of Conflict" as a way of demonstrating that people engage in conflict "either because they have needs that are met by the conflict process itself or because they have needs they can only attain (or believe they can only attain) by engaging in conflict."[1]

Where Burton defines "deeply rooted conflict" as a frustration of basic human needs, Mayer, explains that, "Conflict emerges and is experienced along cognitive (perception), emotional (feeling), and behavior (action) dimensions."[2] Assuming a three dimensional perspective to conflict allows for a better understanding of the complex nature of conflict and why conflict often appears to progress in seemingly contradictory directions. In considering conflict as perception, Mayer explains that conflict is a belief that one's own needs, interests, wants, or values are not compatible with the needs, interests, wants, or values of someone else's. There can be both subjective and objective elements to this conflict dimension. As an emotion, conflict can be understood as the actual physiological response a person has to the perception of conflict. This is often described in terms of how this perception makes a person feel — angry, sad, irate, anxious, worried, scared, etc. A conflict may not necessarily manifest behaviorally in order for it to manifest itself emotionally.[3] Emotions and feelings about a conflict may not be felt proportionally by all parties involved. And, of course, our emotions are drivers of our behavior. Conflict is also understood by the actions and words expressed by those who are in conflict. Conflict as behavior may be expressed as a direct action taken by one person or as an exercise of power. It may be a form of violence or a form of conciliation.[4] The action associated with a conflict is often what parties assume the conflict is actually about. Mayer argues that by considering conflict along all three dimensions — cognitive, emotional, and behavioral — it becomes evident that it does not proceed linearly. Each person or group within a conflict is engaging in each dimension differently and with varying intensity, which accounts for what often appears to be irrational and inconsistent behavior by the involved parties.

Like individuals, social systems also experience conflict that can be understood along the social and cognitive dimensions, although as Mayer explains, these are typically understood in terms of *culture, ethos, organizational* (family, community, national) *values, public opinion* and *popular beliefs.*[5]

Understanding the nature of social systems conflicts require that we reconcile the emotive and cognitive nature of them and accept that within social systems conflict evokes certain reactions and attitudes from a significant number of people within a society although not always the majority. Mayer explains that "when we look at conflicts between union and management, environmental groups and industry associations, progressives and conservatives, it is important to understand the attitudes, feelings, values, and beliefs that these groups have concerning each other if we are to understand what is occurring."[6] The way in which — and the degree to which — the individuals within the system perceive the conflict frustrates their basic human needs will have a correlating impact on the intensity of the response to the conflict. In this way, Mayer is in alignment with Burton — at the core of deeply rooted conflict is the frustration of human needs, which may manifest itself as competition for resources and power; expressions of frustration as it relates to the structures and institutions that hold up society; ineffective and flawed communication; and class struggle.

Mayer's "Wheel of Conflict" was designed to function as a practical framework that serves as a map that guides conflict engagers through the conflict process and helps determine what is at the root of a particular conflict. By understanding the different sources of conflict and the forces that motivate conflict behavior, conflict engagers are able to discern the best path forward. The Wheel of Conflict is depicted in Figure 2.[7]

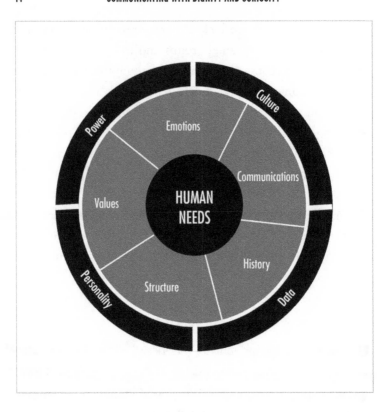

Fig. 2 / Bernard Mayer's Wheel of Conflict

The Wheel of Conflict was derived from, or inspired by, Christopher Moore's "circle of conflict." Mayer explains that Moore's circle of conflict included "relationship problems, data problems, value differences, structural problems and interests"[8] as its core components, all of which were valuable yet incomplete because it failed to incorporate basic human needs, which as Burton asserts, are non-negotiable and always defensible. Mayer also agrees with Burton that human needs are at the core of all deeply rooted conflicts. He explains that,

"People engage in conflict either because they have needs that are met by the conflict process itself or because they have needs that they can only attain (or believe they can only attain) by engaging in conflict."[9] Human needs must be addressed in order for the conflict to be transformed.

To be effective in addressing needs, conflict engagers typically will need to work through the elements that influence how people experience their needs and how they pursue them. Mayer has identified five factors that are particularly critical to understanding how conflict unfolds. These are represented in the wheel: the ways in which people communicate, their emotions, their values, the structures in which they interact, and history.[10]

Emotions

Emotions are physiological and can be objectively measured by blood flow, brain activity, facial micro-expressions and body language. Feelings are how we experience our emotions based off the memory associations and reactions we have with that emotion. Feelings are subjective and are influenced by personal experiences, beliefs, personal temperament and memories. In conflict, our emotions can be stimulated, or triggered, by the ways in which, and the degree to which, our human needs are frustrated. We express these emotions through a range of feelings such as anger, sadness, anxiety, worry, etc. Our emotions are the energy that drives conflict, and they can also be the energy that serves to de-escalate it. A skilled conflict engager is able to help those in conflict manage and regulate their emotional experiences and emotional expressions.

Communication

Humans are imperfect communicators and are especially challenged when experiencing emotional duress. When human needs are frustrated, it is not always apparent or obvious to the person that they are experiencing a form of violence or that they are experiencing a violation of a human need. They may experience strong emotions, express those emotions through bold or overtly communicated feelings, but they are often very challenged to convey effectively about what is driving the emotion. In other words, people are often not adept at identifying or articulating their needs. Add to this complexity, the fact that culture, gender, age, class, cognitive capacity, and environment all influence conflict and communication.

Honing one's emotional intelligence skills is crucial to increasing one's communication skills. The proficient conflict engager is able to help those in conflict unpack their emotional experiences, and communicate them in a manner that moves the conflict forward productively.

History

Conflict must be understood within its historical context. As Mayer explains, "The history of participants in a conflict, of the system in which the conflict is occurring, and the issues themselves has a powerful influence on the course of that conflict. ... History provides the momentum for the development of conflict."[11] History offers insight into how and why human needs have become frustrated; and therefore, understanding the history of a conflict also enables the conflict engager to envision a path forward — one that may be amenable to all parties and that honors the human needs of the parties as well as the unique needs of the social system.

Structure

The structure is the framework in which interactions takes place and complications develop and is, therefore, another potential source of conflict. Structural components of conflict may include "available resources, decision-making procedures, time constraints, legal requirements, communications mechanisms, and physical settings."[12] Although structural elements may be altered as a result of a conflict process, often the structure in which a conflict arises is unalterable, and the parties must find a means of achieving resolution within the existing system. However, if the structure is the source of the frustrated human need, a change in the system will be required in order to achieve a transformation of the conflict.

Values

"Values are the beliefs we have about what is important, what distinguishes right from wrong and good from evil, and what principles should govern how we lead our lives."[13] Values are deeply associated with one's sense of self and sense of integrity.

Therefore, when a person perceives that his or her values are under attacked, it is experienced as though the person's identity is under attack. An identity attack can feel as real as a physical attack, causing the amygdala to respond, adrenaline to flood the system, and the "fight or flight" survival response to kick in. Conflicts that are oriented around values can quickly become intractable and emotionally charged, making communication increasingly more difficult. Mayer asserts that, "When individuals address values directly and express their beliefs affirmatively, they can address conflict more constructively."[14] This often requires the assistance of sophisticated conflict engager who is comfortable navigating an emotional landscape that is not always predictable or comfortable.

Contextual Factors

Mayer's "Wheel of Conflict" also includes contextual factors that influence all sources of conflict — culture, power, personality, and data.

Humans have a unique way of making sense of the world. We absorb stimuli from the outside world and then transform that stimuli into symbols. With our minds, we deconstruct the outside world into a mass of mental symbols, and then recombine those symbols to recreate the world as we perceived it. What we the respond to is often the mental construct of the stimulus, rather than the actual experiences themselves. Of course, each recreation differs from person to person. Our recreations are the mechanisms from which we build identity. The recreations also differ from group to group and from society to society, hence the mechanism for how we build community. Ultimately, this recreation of stimulus into symbols, and the myriad meaning we give to it influences the conflict and disagreements that we encounter.

As we go about the business of deconstructing the outside world into a mass of mental symbols, and recombine those symbols to recreate the world, we utilize culture a as a means of filtering our understanding of the stimulus. Culture can be understood as the social behavior and norms found in human societies. Culture includes a person's values, beliefs, customs, languages and traditions. Through our culture we develop a sense of belonging, personal and cognitive growth and the ability to empathize and relate to each other. Culture can be thought of as the software of the mind. As we perceive symbols and other stimuli from the outside world, this "software" serves as a filter for how we recombine those symbols to recreate the outside world.

Culture encompasses the range of phenomena that are passed on through social learning in all human societies. Culture clearly influences conflict because it plays a role in communication styles, history, emotional expression, values development, and the structure of conflict. Power can be understood as one's ability to influence the behavior of others. Understanding the power dynamics between the parties in conflict or within the social system is paramount to navigating a conflict in which human needs are frustrated.

Personality too can be a source of conflict largely as it relates to interpersonal styles, emotional expressions, and the ways in which a person utilizes power and data to navigate conflict and achieve his or needs.

Human Needs in Conflict

Mayer's concept of human needs differs from John Burton's Basic Human Needs Theory. Mayer's human needs more closely resemble Maslow's theory, though he too does not hold the position that they are hierarchical. Also, Mayer makes a point to differentiate between interests and needs. Mayer explained that, "Interests are viewed as more transitory and superficial, needs as more basic and enduring."[15] Some conflict theorists argue that resolutions that focus primarily on interests versus needs are less enduring.

Mayer proposes that human needs are considered via three overlapping types of needs that are present in conflict and that provide insight into the core of motivations of behavior in conflict. Mayer categorizes human needs in conflict under three main brackets: 1) survival needs; 2) interests; and 3) identity needs.[16] (See Figure 3)

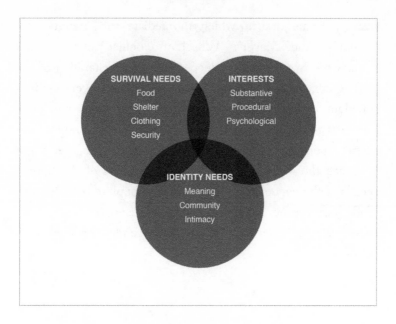

Fig. 3 / Bernard Mayer's Human Needs in Conflict

A fundamental difference between John Burton's Basic Human Needs Theory and Bernard Mayer's Human Needs in Conflict is at the level of implementation.

Burton drafted a list of human needs that are core to deeply rooted conflicts — those conflicts that cannot be negotiated because the source is founded in the violation or deprivation of essential, ontological human needs. Mayer's "human needs in conflict" seem to be designed with mediated interventions in mind — i.e., what Burton would call *disputes* as opposed to *deeply rooted conflicts*.

While Burton's Human Needs Theory is more reflective of comprehensive human needs, Mayer offer's a legitimate and worthy framework in which to mediate the resolution of disputes. And, Mayer's "Wheel of Conflict" offers a vital framework from which to deepen one's understanding of the full context of a conflict or dispute and therefore engage in a problem-solving process in which one seeks to deepen one's understanding of all parties' perspectives, needs, hopes, and desires more thoroughly. Therefore, the conflict engager might embrace the Wheel of Conflict and conceive of the human needs at the center as an opportunity to explore both Mayer's and Burton's human needs interchangeably depending on whether one is seeking to transform conflict or mediate a dispute.

4

THE DIGNITY MODEL

International peace-builder Donna Hicks developed what she refers to as "The Dignity Model" based on her multi-disciplinary research and two decades' experience working with warring parties around the globe. What she discovered is that the concept of dignity is the missing link in understanding human conflict. Through her research and professional experience, she determined humans are particularly vulnerable to being treated as if they didn't matter, and that treatment or disregard wounds something very profound in the human spirit. She argues that this vulnerability "explains why it hurts when our dignity is violated, and it gives us the knowledge, awareness, and skills to avoid unknowingly harming others."[1]

Understanding the role of dignity in the human experience enables us to repair and rebuild relationships that have been broken as a result of conflict and illuminates paths to reconciliation. She explains that by honoring the dignity of others, people are able to experience the freedom necessary to invite intimacy and connection.

The overarching message of "The Dignity Model" is: "Demonstrate the care and attention for yourself and others that anything of value deserves."[2] Hicks asserts that humans share a longing for dignity that when experienced and recognized in one another creates a sense of safety for all parties, which is necessary for growth and development in the relationship to occur.

Dignity is so vital to the human experience that when a person's dignity is violated that violation is experienced similarly to the way the brain processes a physical threat. The amygdala can become triggered and the person may experience the fight or flight response.

In her book, *Dignity: The essential role in resolving conflict*, Hicks writes:[3]

Thus, what appears to exist side by side with human desire for dignity is an opposing tension: our obvious vulnerability. Although we are precious and invaluable beings, our dignity can be violated very quickly, just as our lives can be upended in the blink of an eye. We are just as vulnerable to feeling unworthy as we are to feeling worthy. Because of the primacy of our relationships, our sensitivity to others and the world leaves us open to injury of all sorts and, ultimately, to the possibility of death. It appears that the feeling of loss is at the heart of human vulnerability — loss of dignity, loss of connection to others, and loss of life itself.

The experience of worth and vulnerability is an emotional experience that is derived from the limbic system. Therefore, our responses to dignity violations are also rooted in emotions and a myriad destabilizing feelings that cause us to experience pain and aversion such as dread, shame, anger, disgust.

Most people will go to great lengths to avoid these negative feelings. Hicks notes that, "Some people who have experienced chronic violations of dignity have even gone to the extreme of taking their own lives to bring an end to these intolerable feelings. Others go to the opposite extreme by killing those who caused the injury."[4]

The human brain is wired for connection and dignity plays a crucial role in fostering connection. So, while the limbic system supports survival by producing hormones in the amygdala that serve as a means of self-protection (cortisol and adrenaline) and fuels the body's ability to fight or flee the scene of danger, it also supports human connection by eliciting oxytocin and other feel good hormones that support human connection, bonding, and trust. And dignity plays a crucial role here as well. The more we honor, support, and encourage the intrinsic value in others, the more we are able to connect with them, and these social connections build upon one another in positive and prosocial ways. Hicks explains:[5]

Being treated with dignity triggers the limbic system to release those pleasant feelings of being seen, recognized, and valued — all the life-expanding experiences that come with human connection. Instead of being flooded with fear, anger, resentment, and revenge, we experience safety in a new way. After treating one another with dignity repeatedly, after having multiple reciprocal experiences of recognizing another's value and vulnerability, we will be well on our way to discovering the possibilities that lie before us. With our inner worlds free from the turmoil and uncertainty that accompany our fear of loss of dignity, we can explore a new frontier together, what it is like to feel safe enough to be vulnerable.

So, while the brain has two innate ways in which to seek safety and ensure survival, self-preservation seems to have been the dominant default mode of survival which has resulted in myriad conflicts and wide spread human-inflicted suffering throughout history. Hick's dignity model offers the possibility of a paradigm shift — a roadmap for a new way of being in relation with one another.

The Dignity Model also offers a proactive approach to peace-building, an approach that cultivates peace as way a of *being* rather than as a response to conflict. The Dignity Model is a framework for proactively creating and sustaining peace, as well as a reactive model for responding to conflict.

"The Dignity Model" is rather straight forward. Hicks has identified ten essential elements that are critical to a person's dignity and that serve as a guide for how to communicate with and treat others. It is critical to become familiar with the ten essentials elements of dignity, because only by knowing what they are can people develop the awareness necessary to ensure they do not unintentionally violate the dignity of others.

Although we innately know when our dignity has b
we do not innately understand why or know wh
ensure we do not violate the dignity of others.

Donna Hick's "Ten Essential Elements of Dignity" are as follows:[6]

1. **Acceptance of identity**. Approach people as being neither inferior nor superior to you. Give others the freedom to express their authentic selves without fear of being negatively judged. Interact without prejudice or bias, accepting the ways in which race, religion, ethnicity, gender, class, sexual orientation, age, and disability may be at the core of other people's identities. Assume that others have integrity.

2. **Inclusion**. Make others feel that they belong, whatever the relationship — whether they are in your family, community, organization, or nation.

3. **Safety**. Put people at ease at two levels: physically, so they feel safe from bodily harm, and psychologically, so they feel safe from being humiliated. Help them to feel free to speak without fear of retribution.

4. **Acknowledgement**. Give people your full attention by listening, hearing, validating, and responding to their concerns, feelings, and experiences.

5. **Recognition**. Validate others for their talent, hard work, thoughtfulness, and help. Be generous with praise, and show appreciation and gratitude to others for their contributions.

6. **Fairness**. Treat people justly, with equality, and in

an even-handed way according to agreed-on laws and rules. People feel that you have honored their dignity when you treat them without discrimination or injustice.

7. **Benefit of the doubt**. Treat people as trustworthy. Start with the premise that others have good motives and are acting with integrity.

8. **Understanding**. Believe that what others think matters. Give them the chance to explain and express their point of view. Actively listen in order to understand them.

9. **Independence**. Encourage people to act on their own behalf so that they feel in control of their lives and experience a sense of hope and possibility.

10. **Accountability**. Take responsibility for your actions. If you have violated the dignity of another person, apologize. Make a commitment to change your hurtful behaviors.

Hicks derived the essential elements of dignity through her own observations while facilitating dialogues between warring parties. It became clear that unaddressed violations of dignity was the key factor that prevented parties from coming together in agreement. In other words, it was the emotions they felt and the feelings they expressed toward one another as a direct result of the treatment of one another that created a barrier to resolution and not their ability to achieve common ground.

Hicks had been trained in John Burton's Basic Human Needs Theory as well as Herbert Kelman's interactive problem-solving approach, which seeks to assist parties in deepening their understandings of one another. Problems become solvable when parties are capable of conceiving one another as equals as it relates to their shared human needs.

Hicks explains that the "Burton-Kelman approach focused on providing a forum for parties to discuss unmet needs, the insights from which could be fed into the political process."[7] What she realized in this process of facilitating complex dialogues between staunch enemies is that Burton's initial list was lacking key elements of dignity, such as:[8]

- The desire to be understood
- The desire for suffering to be named and acknowledged
- The desire to be freed from domination so that space for hope and possibility could grow
- The desire to be given the benefit of a doubt
- The desire to be apologized to when wronged

Ultimately, the ten essential elements of dignity built on Burton's original needs and operationalized the concept of dignity — something Hicks had determined was essential to truly transforming deeply rooted conflicts.

5

ENGAGING IN CONFLICT WITH DIGNITY AND CURIOSITY

John Burton, Bernie Mayer, Donna Hicks and the countless conflict theorists who informed and shaped their thinking have had a tremendous influence on my understanding of deeply rooted conflict and how to build systems of sustainable peace — systems that have the potential to truly transform the human experience. What was missing for me in my research was how to take this knowledge and make it actionable from the perspective of truly engaging parties in a manner that acknowledges and honors human needs, including the need for dignity. I began a search for a framework that allowed the freedom and space to bring these concepts to life and that allowed facilitators and parties of conflict to engage in a way that supported the key functions of peace — human security and the ability to live a life of dignity that is free of fear.

As Donna Hicks noted in her book, *Dignity,* the default response for most people who have been on the receiving end of a dignity violation is shame, humiliation, dread, etc. These feelings do not lend themselves to learning. When we are on the defense and experiencing a fight or flight response, our focus is on surviving the assault. What is needed is a framework that supports a brain-sensitive learning environment. In other words, a communication framework that encourages curiosity, awareness of self and others, and that shifts the focus from blame, judgment and shame to collaboration and understanding. In their book, *The Power of Curiosity: How to Have Real Conversations That Create Collaboration, Innovation, and Understanding*, executive coaches Kathy Taberner and Kirsten Taberner Siggins offer a simple framework oriented around honing one's curiosity skills. One reason this framework is so effective for engaging in dialogues about deeply rooted conflicts is its focus on curiosity.

Research in the field of neuroscience confirms that when a person experiences curiosity, the hormones dopamine and oxytocin are released in the brain. These feel good hormones support us in connecting with each other because they create a connection between the prefrontal cortex and the limbic system — the brain and the heart — that allows people to experience a greater sense of openness. Consequently, a new shared understanding is able to emerge and along with that a new shared reality.[1]

Curiosity is a frontal lobe activity. Important functions of the prefrontal cortex, located in the frontal lobe, are reasoning, problem-solving, and decision-making. Because curiosity is a frontal lobe activity and anger, shame, anxiety, etc. are functions of the limbic system, it is almost impossible to be mad and curious at the same time, which means curiosity is a brain-sensitive learning skill. If we are able to maintain curiosity about another person's behavior, we are less likely to internalize it and more apt to explore what is driving the behavior. As we gain understanding about the driving forces behind a person's behavior, our capacity to experience compassion for them grows and our ability to extend empathy toward them is also enhanced. Through curiosity, compassion, and empathy, we are able to begin to transcend conflict and peaceful paths forward begin to emerge.

Like "The Dignity Model," the framework for cultivating curiosity skills is quite straightforward. However, Taberner and Taberner Siggins present the information in a very helpful manner that allows for a step-by-step approach with a lack of rigidity that might render it theoretical but not implementable. Below (Figure 4) is a visual rendering of Taberner and Taberner Siggins' framework for cultivating curiosity skills slightly revised.[2]

While it is obvious that this framework is not a linear process, but rather three actions to take (or three ways of *being*) as one moves through a dialogue process. What I appreciate most about this framework is its simplicity. I have taken the liberty to revise the framework slightly and bring my own insights that I have gathered along my educational and professional journey to this framework.

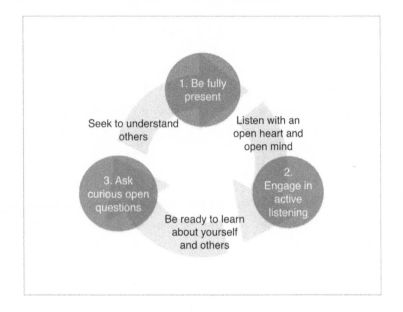

Fig. 4 / Cultivating Curiosity Skills

Step One

The first "step" in the process is to be fully present. This is both an instruction to the dialogue facilitator and the participants. When we are fully present, we are intentional about being authentic and bringing our most heartfelt and sincere self to the discussion. We listen empathetically and without judgment for the message hidden beneath the words. We offer the truth as we understand it in the current moment without blame or judgment. We exercise emotional intelligence skills and maintain awareness, to the best of our ability, about the impact our personality, culture, gender, and overall communication style may have on the other parties and the process. And, perhaps most importantly, we listen for the unmet needs that are being expressed through the emotions and feelings of those with whom we may be experiencing conflict.

Step Two

The second "step" is to choose how to listen. There is a time for gaining understanding and there is a time for problem-solving. Knowing what is required of us at each stage of a dialogue is necessary and will inform the way in which we choose to listen. Regardless of whether we are listening to problem-solve or listening to gain understanding, utilizing active listening skills is of paramount importance.

Active listening is a method of listening and responding attentively with the intent of building rapport and trust while deepening one's understanding of the other person. The goal of active listening is to deepen one's connection to the person with whom communication is occurring and to gain a richer understanding of the speaker's feelings and needs and to begin to "hear" a request even when one is not directly spoken.[3] Approaches to active listening include, but are not limited to, the following:[4]

- Acknowledging
- Clarifying
- Encouraging
- Normalizing
- Reframing
- Summarizing

- Supplementing
- Validating

An obvious element of active listening is being mindful of what might be blocking us for doing so. Below are some common blocks to listening. Of course, this is not an exhaustive list, but it is a starting place for facilitators to recommend parties in dialogue with one another be aware of.[5]

- Comparing
- Mind reading
- Rehearsing
- Filtering
- Judging
- Dreaming
- Identifying
- Advising
- Sparring
- Being right
- Derailing
- Placating
- External noise
- Processing rate
- Information overload
- Not interested in the topic

By being fully present, intentional about how we listen, and engaging in active listening, we will automatically begin to learn more about others and ourselves. Being willing to lean into this new learning, rather than resist it and get rooted in our previous thinking is critical.

. . .

Step Three

Asking open and curious questions is how we lean in to conflict and deepen our understanding of every aspect of it. Curiosity engaged our frontal lobe, the area of the brain responsible for logic, reasoning, and decision-making. Curiosity invites collaboration, problem-solving, and even compassion. Examples of curious questions include, but certainly are not limited to:

- Can you tell me more about that feeling, belief, perspective, etc.?
- What experiences have you had that have shaped your thinking as it relates to this feeling, belief, perspective, etc.?
- If you were to peel back all the layers, what is at the root of this issue for you?
- Why does this feeling, belief, issue, etc. move you so deeply?
- Do you see any contradictions or paradoxes in your thinking about this particular issue?
- What underlying values or ethical beliefs have shaped your thinking?
- What needs are you seeking to fulfill through this action?

When we lean into conflict with curiosity, we automatically invite the same from others. Our curiosity has the power to transform a conflict conversation into a learning conversation. And models a path for others to follow.

6

BRINGING IT ALL TOGETHER

I n my work as a conflict engager, I have been most interested in gaining an understanding of how to develop systems of sustainable peace — systems that function proactively as well as retroactively.

Remember, peace is *human security and the ability to live a life of dignity that is free of fear.* So, a framework that cultivates peace must be grounded in the acknowledgment, honoring and preservation of human needs while also recognizing and honoring the role of dignity in all human interactions. Lastly, we need to be able to engage one another through peaceful means when tensions surface.

Burton's Basic Human Needs Theory, Mayer's Wheel of Conflict, and Hick's Dignity Model paired with Taberner and Taberner Siggins' curiosity skills all function together in a comprehensive, logical, and exciting framework for cultivating and sustaining peace within any system — families, school, workplaces, communities, and nations.

Utilizing these core theories, I have developed the Communicating With Curiosity and Dignity framework that works to proactively promote peace, as well as engage in conflict through peaceful means when conflict surfaces. This model is designed to ensure human security and dignity at all stages of engagement. Figure 5 provides a visual illustration of how each theory works together to create a framework for peace-building.

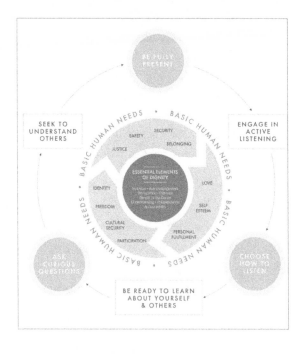

Fig. 5 / Communicating With Curiosity and Dignity

At the center of the model are the ten essentials of dignity. As Hick's and others researchers have demonstrated, any threat to our dignity is perceived as a physical threat. Paramount to peace-building is the recognition, acknowledgement, and preservation of a person's inherent worth and value as a human being. It is the first stepping stone toward any path of peace. Wrapping around this nucleus of dignity is the recognition of and honoring of Basic Human Needs. The outside layer represents the communication module — a methodology for engaging in conflict through dialogue when parties are experiencing deeply rooted conflict as well disputes that can be successfully resolved through interest-based negotiations.

As a conflict specialist and peace-building trainer, I am beginning to carve out an interesting and unique niche working with organizations that operate in a flat structure — organizations that distribute authority and decision-making throughout the organization and that define the individuals working in the organization not by hierarchy and titles, but rather by roles. In these organizations, the intent is to honor the whole person and allow them to contribute from the fullness of their knowledge, expertise, and passion. And yet, the individuals do not have a cognitive map for relating with one another in the workplace with such a high level of transparency and collaboration. Conflict, sometimes deeply rooted conflict, is the result. The implementation of the "Communicating With Curiosity and Dignity Model" within these organizations has given them shared knowledge, language, and processes from which to communicate and engage with one another and that honors the organizations' desire to create a culture that embraces the wholeness of the individuals within the workforce. Recognizable shifts occur in the cultures of these organizations and in the interpersonal relationships within the workforce, which creates a shift within the system itself.

I invite you to utilize the Communicating With Curiosity and

Dignity framework as you explore more peaceful approaches to not just navigating conflict, but also in developing systems of sustainable peace within your workplace, communities of faith, homes, and in any other system in which you regular engage.

NOTES

2. BASIC HUMAN NEEDS THEORY

1. Avruch, Kevin, and C. R. Mitchell. "Basic Human Need in Theory and Practice." *Conflict Resolution and Human Needs: Linking Theory and Practice*, Routledge, 2014, pp. 1–3

2. Avruch, Kevin, and C. R. Mitchell. "Basic Human Need in Theory and Practice." *Conflict Resolution and Human Needs: Linking Theory and Practice*, Routledge, 2014, pp. 4

3. Galtung, Johan. "Violence, Peace, and Peace Research." *Journal of Peace Research*, vol. 6, no. 3, 1969, pp. 167–191., doi:10.1177/002234336900600301.

4. Avruch, Kevin, and C. R. Mitchell. "Basic Human Need in Theory and Practice." *Conflict Resolution and Human Needs: Linking Theory and Practice*, Routledge, 2014, pp. 6

5. Avruch, Kevin, and C. R. Mitchell. "Basic Human Need in Theory and Practice." *Conflict Resolution and Human Needs: Linking Theory and Practice*, Routledge, 2014, pp. 8

6. Avruch, Kevin, and C. R. Mitchell. "Basic Human Need in Theory and Practice." *Conflict Resolution and Human Needs: Linking Theory and Practice*, Routledge, 2014, pp. 8

7. Sandole, Dennis J.D. "Extending the Reach of Basic Human Needs: A Comprehensive Theory for the Twenty-First Century." *Conflict Resolution and Human Needs: Linking Theory and Practice*, by Kevin Avruch and C. R. Mitchell, Routledge, 2014, pp. 22.

8. Sandole, Dennis J.D. "Extending the Reach of Basic Human Needs: A Comprehensive Theory for the Twenty-First Century." *Conflict Resolution and Human Needs: Linking Theory and Practice*, by Kevin Avruch and C. R. Mitchell, Routledge, 2014, pp. 23.

9. Sandole, Dennis J.D. "Extending the Reach of Basic Human Needs: A Comprehensive Theory for the Twenty-First Century." *Conflict Resolution and Human Needs: Linking Theory and Practice*, by Kevin Avruch and C. R. Mitchell, Routledge, 2014, pp. 23.

10. Ibid.

11. Sandole, Dennis J.D. "Extending the Reach of Basic Human Needs: A Comprehensive Theory for the Twenty-First Century." *Conflict Resolution*

and Human Needs: Linking Theory and Practice, by Kevin Avruch and C. R. Mitchell, Routledge, 2014, pp. 24.

12. Ibid.

13. Part I: Peace Studies: An Epistemological Basis." *Peace by Peaceful Means: Peace and Conflict, Development and Civilization*, by Johan Galtung, Prio, 2012, pp. 9–9.

14. Sandole, Dennis J.D. "Extending the Reach of Basic Human Needs: A Comprehensive Theory for the Twenty-First Century." *Conflict Resolution and Human Needs: Linking Theory and Practice*, by Kevin Avruch and C. R. Mitchell, Routledge, 2014, pp. 24-25

15. Sandole, Dennis J.D. "Extending the Reach of Basic Human Needs: A Comprehensive Theory for the Twenty-First Century." *Conflict Resolution and Human Needs: Linking Theory and Practice*, by Kevin Avruch and C. R. Mitchell, Routledge, 2014, pp. 25

16. Sandole, Dennis J.D. "Extending the Reach of Basic Human Needs: A Comprehensive Theory for the Twenty-First Century." *Conflict Resolution and Human Needs: Linking Theory and Practice*, by Kevin Avruch and C. R. Mitchell, Routledge, 2014, pp. 25

3. WHEEL OF CONFLICT

1. Mayer, Bernard S. *The Dynamics of Conflict: a Guide to Engagement and Intervention.* Jossey-Bass, 2012.

2. The Nature of Conflict." *The Dynamics of Conflict: a Guide to Engagement and Intervention*, by Bernard S. Mayer, Jossey-Bass, 2012, pp. 4–4.

3. The Nature of Conflict." *The Dynamics of Conflict: a Guide to Engagement and Intervention*, by Bernard S. Mayer, Jossey-Bass, 2012, pp. 5–5.

4. The Nature of Conflict." *The Dynamics of Conflict: a Guide to Engagement and Intervention*, by Bernard S. Mayer, Jossey-Bass, 2012, pp. 6–6.

5. The Nature of Conflict." *The Dynamics of Conflict: a Guide to Engagement and Intervention*, by Bernard S. Mayer, Jossey-Bass, 2012, pp. 7–7.

6. The Nature of Conflict." *The Dynamics of Conflict: a Guide to Engagement and Intervention*, by Bernard S. Mayer, Jossey-Bass, 2012, pp. 8–8.

7. The Nature of Conflict." *The Dynamics of Conflict: a Guide to Engagement and Intervention*, by Bernard S. Mayer, Jossey-Bass, 2012, pp. 10–10.

8. The Nature of Conflict." *The Dynamics of Conflict: a Guide to Engagement and Intervention*, by Bernard S. Mayer, Jossey-Bass, 2012, pp. 10–10.

9. The Nature of Conflict." *The Dynamics of Conflict: a Guide to Engagement and Intervention*, by Bernard S. Mayer, Jossey-Bass, 2012, pp. 11–11.

10. Ibid.

11. The Nature of Conflict." *The Dynamics of Conflict: a Guide to Engagement and Intervention*, by Bernard S. Mayer, Jossey-Bass, 2012, pp. 17–17.

12. The Nature of Conflict." *The Dynamics of Conflict: a Guide to Engagement and Intervention*, by Bernard S. Mayer, Jossey-Bass, 2012, pp. 16–16.

13. The Nature of Conflict." *The Dynamics of Conflict: a Guide to Engagement and Intervention*, by Bernard S. Mayer, Jossey-Bass, 2012, pp. 14–14.

14. The Nature of Conflict." *The Dynamics of Conflict: a Guide to Engagement and Intervention*, by Bernard S. Mayer, Jossey-Bass, 2012, pp. 16–16.

15. The Nature of Conflict." *The Dynamics of Conflict: a Guide to Engagement and Intervention*, by Bernard S. Mayer, Jossey-Bass, 2012, pp. 21–21.

16. The Nature of Conflict." *The Dynamics of Conflict: a Guide to Engagement and Intervention*, by Bernard S. Mayer, Jossey-Bass, 2012, pp. 21–21.

4. THE DIGNITY MODEL

1. Introduction [Introduction]. (2013). In D. Hicks (Author), *Dignity: Its essential role in resolving conflict* (pp. 2-3). New Haven: Yale University Press.

2. Introduction [Introduction]. (2013). In D. Hicks (Author), *Dignity: Its essential role in resolving conflict* (pp. 2-3). New Haven: Yale University Press.

3. Introduction [Introduction]. (2013). In D. Hicks (Author), *Dignity: Its essential role in resolving conflict* (pp. 7-7). New Haven: Yale University Press.

4. Introduction [Introduction]. (2013). In D. Hicks (Author), *Dignity: Its essential role in resolving conflict* (pp. 7-7). New Haven: Yale University Press.

5. Ibid.

6. Hicks, D. (2013). Part one: The ten essential elements of dignity. In *Dignity: Its essential role in resolving conflict* (pp. 25-26). New Haven: Yale University Press

7. Hicks, D. (2013). Part one: The ten essential elements of dignity. In *Dignity: Its essential role in resolving conflict* (pp. 27-27). New Haven: Yale University Press

8. Hicks, D. (2013). Part one: The ten essential elements of dignity. In *Dignity: Its essential role in resolving conflict* (pp. 28-28). New Haven: Yale University Press

5. ENGAGING IN CONFLICT WITH DIGNITY AND CURIOSITY

1. Taberner, K., & Siggins, K. T. (2015). *The power of curiosity: How to have real conversations that create collaboration, innovation and understanding.* New York: Morgan James.

2. Taberner, K., & Siggins, K. T. (2015). *The power of curiosity: How to have real conversations that create collaboration, innovation and understanding.* New York: Morgan James.

3. Short, R. (2016). *Peace in the workplace: Transforming conflict into collaboration.* Dallas, TX: GoodMedia Press.

4. Ibid.

5. Short, R. (2016). *Peace in the workplace: Transforming conflict into collaboration.* Dallas, TX: GoodMedia Press.

ABOUT THE AUTHOR

Robyn Short is an international peace-building trainer and mediator with expertise in restorative justice and transformative mediation models. She works with individuals, corporations, and nonprofit organizations in discovering the root causes of their conflicts, so they may transform their relationships and create new and productive paths forward individually and as teams. She also works with community leaders and political and governmental leaders to develop grassroots efforts for building sustainable peace in areas of historic conflict. In this capacity, she has been featured in news outlets internationally.

Robyn is the author of four books and the founder and publisher of GoodMedia Press, an independent publishing house that's mission is to actively and passionately promote peace and social justice through books and other media.

In addition to her mediation and conflict training practice, Robyn is an adjunct professor at Southern Methodist University in the Master of Conflict Management and Dispute Resolution program, the Master of Leadership and Negotiation at Bay Path University, and El Centro Conflict Management program. She is a frequent guest lecturer at Pepperdine University and Creighton University.

Robyn is currently a Liberal Studies doctoral candidate at Southern Methodist University. She holds a Master in Conflict Management and Dispute Resolution from Southern Methodist University and a Master of Liberal Studies from Southern Methodist University with a focus in 15th century European History. She holds a Bachelor of Science in Psychology from Auburn University.